HILARIOUS JOKES

FOR

YEAR OLD KIDS

A Message From the Publisher

Hello! My name is Hayden and I am the owner of Hayden Fox Publishing, the publishing house that brought you this title.

My hope is that you and your young comedian love this book and enjoy every single page. If you do, please think about **giving us your honest feedback via a review on Amazon**. It may only take a moment, but it really does mean the world for small businesses like mine.

Even if you happen to not like this title, please let us know the reason in your review so that we may improve this title for the future and serve you better.

The mission of Hayden Fox is to create premium content for children that will help them increase their confidence and grow their imaginations while having tons of fun along the way.

Without you, however, this would not be possible, so we sincerely thank you for your purchase and for supporting our company mission.

Sincerely,
Hayden Fox

Why does a giraffe have a long neck?

Because his feet stink.

What do you get if you cross a frog with a rabbit?

A bunny ribbit.

---: DID YOU KNOW? :---

★ The average star is between 1 and 10 billion years old
(although some are even older!) ★

 One million Earths could fit inside the sun!

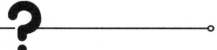

RIDDLES

I have four legs in total, along with a head and a foot.
What am I?
A bed.

Bees hum all the time. Why is this?
They don't know the words.

Sheena leads, Sheila needs.

TONGUE TWISTER

If Stu chews shoes, should Stu choose the shoes he chews?

Knock Knock!

Who's there?
Mikey.
Mikey who?
Mikey doesn't fit in the key hole!

What do you call your dad when he's frozen?

Popsicle

What did the ice cream say to the chocolates?

You're sweet!

$\rightrightarrows$ DID YOU KNOW? $\leftleftarrows$

One day on Venus is almost 4 months on Earth.

 It's impossible to hum while holding your nose.

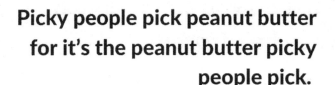

Picky people pick peanut butter for it's the peanut butter picky people pick.

RIDDLES

Why is playing basketball with pigs no fun?
They hog the basketball.

Rabbits love to travel on what machine?
A hare-plane.

--- DID YOU KNOW? ---

 The filling in a Kit Kat is broken up Kit Kats.

Female lions do 90% of the hunting.

 **What's a pirate's favorite restaurant?**

Arrrrby's

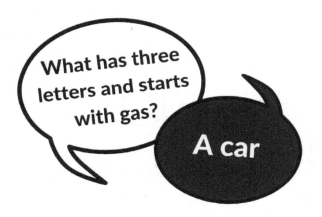

What has three letters and starts with gas?

A car

Who's there?

Ice cream.

Ice cream who?

Ice cream if you don't let me in!

RIDDLES

What is considered black and white but pink all over?
An embarrassed zebra.

Which bank never has any cash or coins?
A riverbank.

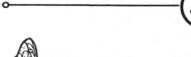
Where do wasps go when they're not feeling well?

The waspital

Knock Knock!

Who's there?
Dime.
Dime who?
Dime to tell another knock-knock joke.

 **Why do vampires brush their teeth?**

They don't want bat breath!

What cereal do mice love to eat?

Micekrispies

DID YOU KNOW?

Chocolate is made from cocoa beans that grow as fruits of the cocoa tree.

 There are over 10,000 different species of birds.

Who's there?
Ike.
Ike who?
Ike-ant stop telling these jokes!

Luke's duck likes lakes.

Luke Luck likes lakes and ducks.

Luke Lake likes his luck on the lake.

Which two things are impossible to have for breakfast?

Lunch and dinner.

 **What do you call a deer that's in the rain?**

A rain deer (reindeer)!

Why did the duck cross the road?

To prove he wasn't chicken!

---: DID YOU KNOW? :---

 If you flew to the Sun from the moon on a plane it would take about 20 years.

 Dogs sneeze when play fighting to show they are just playing and not fighting.

What is the longest word in the dictionary?

"Smiles" because there is a mile between each "S."

RIDDLES

Which word is always spelled incorrectly in the dictionary?

Incorrectly.

Terrible tongue twisters tend to twist.

TONGUE TWISTER

Who's there?

Nose!

Nose who?

She nose more knock knock jokes than me?

Knock Knock!

What do you call a rich elf?

Welfy

How do snails fight?

They slug it out

⌁ DID YOU KNOW? ⌁

The smallest bone in your body is in your ear and it's about as big as a grain of rice.

Some scientists believe that there are aliens already here on Earth...

RIDDLES

I'm never wicked, but I do have a wick. I come in all sizes, from skinny to thick. What am I?

Candle.

Round and round, that's the only way for me! I take with me all your laundry. No need to fret; they're safe with me, for I only want to keep them clean. What am I?

Washing machine.

Who's there?
Cliff.
Cliff who?
Cliff hanger!

Who's there?
Annie.
Annie who?
Annie way you can let me in now?

Why can't you trust the king of the jungle?

He's always LION!

What is a rabbit's favorite dance style?

Hip-Hop!

---≡ DID YOU KNOW? ≡---

A grizzly bear's bite is so strong it can break a bowling ball.

 You can find McDonald's in every continent of the world except Antarctica.

What animal needs oil?
A mouse because it squeaks.

Why did the melon jump into the lake?

It wanted to be a water-melon.

How many cookies could a good cook cook if a good cook could cook cookies?

TONGUE TWISTER

Who's there?
Apple.
Apple who?
Apple your hair if you don't let me in!

Knock Knock!

When you write copy you have the right to copyright the copy you write.

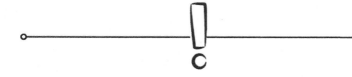

Who's there?

Emma.

Emma who?

Emma bit cold out here, can you let me in?

--- **DID YOU KNOW?** ---

George Washington used to own sheep.

Standing quietly against a wall,
you rarely notice me though I'm tall.
Inside, I keep many treats,
so open my door, and then you'll see!
What am I?
Refrigerator.

I don't go out and play; I just stay at home all day.
I'm nice, you might agree, but mostly your feet just rub me.
What am I?
Doormat.

Why does the sun have to go to school?

To get brighter.

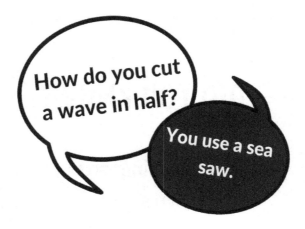

How do you cut a wave in half?

You use a sea saw.

What do you call someone that has no body or nose?

Nobody knows!

What vegetables do librarians like?

Quiet peas

⟶ DID YOU KNOW? ⟵

You have about 100,000 hairs on your head.

Oscar thinks it's really neat but ask another, and they will say it really stinks and should be left on the street. What is it?

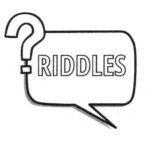

Garbage can.

What do Ninjas eat for dinner?

Kung-food

How much ground would a groundhog ground if a groundhog could hog ground?

Who's there?

Fang.

Fang who?

Fangs for letting me in!

What do you call a skeleton who won't work?

Lazy Bones!

What sound do hedgehogs make when they hug?

Ouch!

-- DID YOU KNOW? --

Jellyfish are made up of 95% water.

The world's largest waterfall is underwater.

For the movie, I shall pop
the corn and when it's ready,
the buzzer will warn. What am I?

Microwave.

What's really easy to get into and
hard to get out of?

Trouble.

Mr. Tongue Twister tried
to train his twisty tongue
to turny twist
and twisty turn.

Who's there?

Ken.

Ken who?

Ken I come in?

What did the frog order at the burger place?

French flies and a diet croak.

DID YOU KNOW?

As of 2018, the world's population has grown to almost 8 billion people.

Pirates wore eye patches to help their eyes get accustomed to seeing in the dark.

We surely shall see the sun shine soon.

Who's there?

Lenny.

Lenny who?

Lenny in the house, please!

Knock Knock!

What wolf got lost in the mall?

The WHEREwolf.

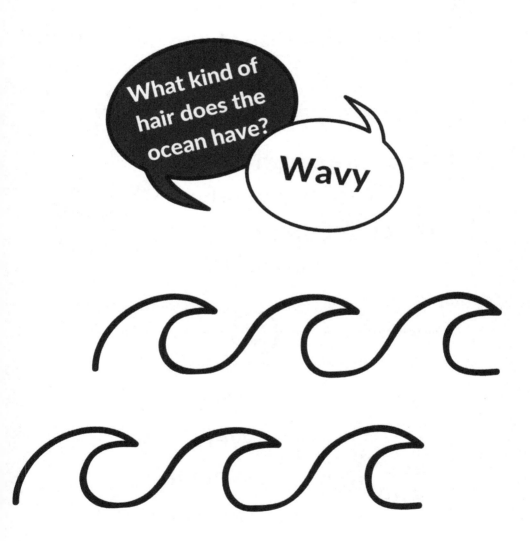

What kind of hair does the ocean have?

Wavy

DID YOU KNOW?

Alpine bumblebees are capable of flying higher than Mount Everest!

It's not the cough that carries you off, it's the coffin they carry you off in!

Who's there?
Wet.
Wet who?
Wet me in, it's waining out here.

What did one egg say to the other?

You crack me up!

What's really fast, really loud, and tastes good with salsa?

A rocket chip!

DID YOU KNOW?

No one really knows who invented the fire hydrant.

Mo me mi me
show me some snow,
me mi mo me
get me a fro.

Who's there?
Dishes.
Dishes who?
Dishes me,
who are you?

 **What did the left eye say to the right eye?**

Between us, something smells!

What did the Dalmatian say after lunch?

That hit the spot!

DID YOU KNOW?

 Strawberries and avocados are actually fruits, not vegetables.

I see a sea down by the seashore. But which sea do you see down by the seashore?

TONGUE TWISTER

Knock Knock!

Who's there?
Will.
Will who?
Will you let me in?
It's freezing out here!

What is a witch's favorite subject in school?

Spelling!

What do you call a duck that gets all A's?

A wise quacker.

--∵- **DID YOU KNOW?** ∵---

 Cats only meow because it's a way of communicating with humans and their mothers.

Strawberries are the only fruits with its seeds on the outside.

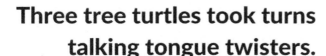

Three tree turtles took turns talking tongue twisters.

 Who's there?
Chuck.
Chuck who?
Chuck and see if the door is locked.

What invention can let people look through walls?

Windows

What falls in winter but never gets hurt?

Snow!

What do you call a ghost's true love?

His ghoul-friend.

I was born on a short and shiny ship at shore.

TONGUE TWISTER

Who's there?

Sarah.

Sarah who?

Sarah dog in there with you!

Knock Knock!

 **What did one volcano say to the other?**

I lava you!

DID YOU KNOW?

 Sea otters hold hands
when they sleep so they don't drift away
from each other.

Mr. Potato Head was the first
toy to be advertised on TV.

Six socks sit in a sink
soaking in soap suds

TONGUE TWISTER

Who's there?

 Goose.

Goose who?

Goose who it is!

How do you get a squirrel to like you?

Act like a nut!

How can you tell a vampire has a cold?

She starts coffin.

What's green and can fly?

Super Pickle!

If a dog chews shoes, whose shoes does he choose?

TONGUE TWISTER

Knock Knock!

Who's there?
Winner.
Winner who?
Winner you gonna get this door fixed?

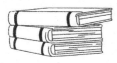 **What do elves learn in school?**

The elf-abet.

DID YOU KNOW?

The surface of Mars is covered in rust, making the planet appear red.

How many yaks could a yak pack pack if a yak pack could pack yaks?

Who's there?
Figs.
Figs who?
Figs your doorbell, it's not working!

Why couldn't the motorcycle stand up?

It was two tired.

What did the wolf say when it stubbed its toe?

Owwwooooo-ch!

DID YOU KNOW?

Several centuries ago in Holland, tulips were more valuable than gold.

Kitty caught the kitten in the kitchen.

TONGUE TWISTER

No need to light a night-light on a night like tonight.

Who's there?
Boo.
Boo, who?
Don't cry, it's just me!

Knock Knock!

What does an evil hen lay?

Deviled eggs.

What does a book do in the winter?

Puts on a jacket.

DID YOU KNOW?

Fleas can jump up to seven inches and more than 80 times their height.

Knock Knock!

Who's there?
Tinker Bell.
Tinker Bell who?
Tinker Bell is out of order!

Give papa a cup of proper coffee in a copper coffee cup.

TONGUE TWISTER

If two witches were watching two watches, which witch would watch which watch?

What kind of haircuts do bees get?

Buzzzzzcuts.

--- **DID YOU KNOW?** ---

Every day, your heart produces enough energy to power a truck for 20 miles.

Violin bows are made from horse hair.

Who's there?

Too short.

Too short who?

Too short to reach the doorbell!

Knock Knock!

Four fine fresh fish for you

Fresh French fried fly fritters

What do you do if you get peanut butter on your doorknob?

Use a door jam.

DID YOU KNOW?

The Queen has two birthdays.

 Most insects hatch from eggs.

Who's there?
Your mom
Your mom who?
Your mom! Now open the door or you're grounded.

Knock Knock!

The soldier's shoulder surely hurts!

 **Where do elephants pack their clothes?**

In their trunks!

**Knock Knock!**

Who's there?
Yelp.
Yelp who?
Yelp me, my nose is
stuck in the keyhole!

**Knock Knock!**

Who's there?
Witches.
Witches who?
Witches the way to go
home?

The greener green grapes are,
the keener keen apes
are to gobble green grape cakes.

TONGUE TWISTER

What part of the fish weighs the most?

The scales.

Who's there?

Bacon.

Bacon who?

Bacon a cake for the party!

Who's there?

A herd.

A herd who?

A herd you the first time.

**How much dew
does a dewdrop drop
if dewdrops do drop dew?**

TONGUE TWISTER

What does a cloud wear under his raincoat?

Thunderwear!

Who's there?
Tank.
Tank who?
You're welcome!

Who's there?
Kanga.
Kanga who?
No, Kangaroo!

No nose knows like a gnome's nose knows.

Each Easter Eddie eats eighty Easter eggs.

What word starts with the letter t, ends with the letter t, and has t in it?

A teapot!

What has four wheels and flies?

A garbage truck!

Who's there?
Some bunny.
Some bunny who?
Some bunny has been eating all my carrots!

Who's there?
Baby owl.
Baby owl who?
Baby owl see you later, maybe I won't!

Whether the weather be fine
or whether the weather be not.
Whether the weather be cold
or whether the weather be hot.
We'll weather the weather
whether we like it or not.

 **What do you call a monkey at the North Pole?**

Lost.

How do cats bake cake?

From scratch.

Knock Knock!

Who's there?
Grrr.
Grrr who?
Are you a polar bear
or an owl?

Knock Knock!

Who's there?
Cat.
Cat who?
Cat you understand!

Mr. See owned a saw and Mr
Soar owned a seesaw.
Now See's saw sawed Soar's
seesaw before Soar saw See.

What is a zombie's favorite thing to eat?

Brain food.

How do you fix a broken tomato?

With a can of tomato paste.

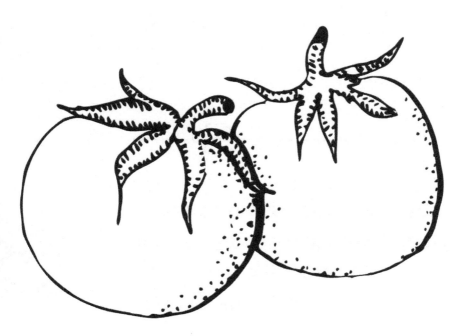

Knock Knock!

Who's there?
Candy.
Candy who?
Candy cow jump
over the moon!

Knock Knock!

Who's there?
Ant.
Ant who?
Ant you glad to see me?

Ray Rag ran across a rough road.
Across a rough road Ray Rag ran.
Where is the rough road
Ray Rag ran across?

TONGUE TWISTER

Why did the skeletons cross the road?

To get to the body shop!

Why was the rabbit happy?

Because some bunny loved him!

Who's there?
Honey bee.
Honey bee who?
Honey bee a sweetie and get me some water.

Who's there?
Roach.
Roach who?
Roach you a letter, did you get it?

I would if I could, and if I couldn't, how could I? You couldn't, unless you could, could you?

What's an astronaut's favorite chocolate bar?

Mars.

What do you call a cat burrito?

A purrito

?

What belongs to you, but other people use it more than you?

Your name.

RIDDLES

What is something you will never see again?

Yesterday.

Knock Knock!

Who's there?
Abby.
Abby who?
Abby good if you give me a candy.

Knock Knock!

Who's there?
Barbie.
Barbie who?
Barbie Q Chicken!

Roberta ran rings around the Roman ruins.

Wayne went to Wales to watch walruses.

Why did the cow lie down in the grass?

He was ground beef.

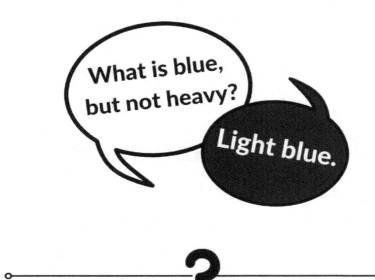

What word has three syllables but contains 26 letters?

Alphabet.

I do not have wings, but I can fly. I do not have eyes, but I can cry. What am I?

A cloud.

Who's there?
Bean.
Bean who?
Bean a while since
I last saw you!

Who's there?
Egg.
Egg who?
Egg-cited to see me?

**There those thousand
thinkers were thinking
how did the other three
thieves go through.**

TONGUE TWISTER

"Doctor, doctor I am afraid of squirrels!"
Doctor: You must be nuts.

What happened to the frog whose car broke down?

He had to be toad!

I do not speak and cannot hear, but I will always tell the truth. What am I?
A mirror.

RIDDLES

I hold lots of memories, but I own nothing. What am I?
A picture frame.

Which word begins and ends with "e" but only contains one letter?

Envelope.

What weighs nothing but not even the world's strongest man can hold it for longer than five minutes?

Breath.

Six sleek swans swam swiftly southwards

Gobbling gargoyles gobbled gobbling goblins.

Why did the tomato stop?

Because he was out of juice.

What do you say when you lose a Wii game?

I want a Wii-match.

?

I was born tall, but as I get older, I become small. What am I?

A candle.

 RIDDLES

If you give me water, I will die, but if you let me be, I will thrive. What am I?

Fire.

Who's there?
Orange.
Orange who?
Orange you glad to see me?

Knock Knock!

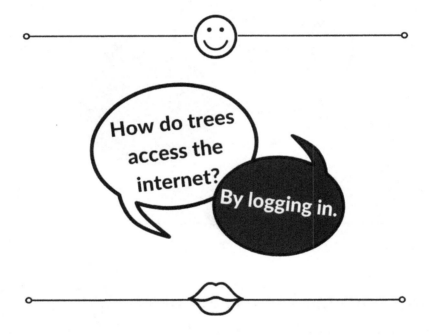

How do trees access the internet?

By logging in.

Elizabeth's birthday is on the third Thursday of this month.

TONGUE TWISTER

Ann and Andy's anniversary is in April.

Mr. Red and Ms. Red live in the red house; Mr. Purple and Ms. Purple live in the purple house. Who lives in the white house?

The president!

On what day of the week do chickens hide?

Fry-day

You can break me without even coming near me. What am I?

A promise.

RIDDLES

It is round on both ends but is high in the middle. What is it?

Ohio

I will always come but will never arrive today. What am I?

Tomorrow.

The farther you walk, the more of me you leave behind. What am I?

Footsteps.

Knock Knock!

Who's there?
Scold
Scold who?
Scold outside!

Mary Mac's mother's making Mary Mac marry me.

TONGUE TWISTER

Why did the chicken cross the road?

It was trying to get away from the KFC.

What kind of music do mummies listen to?

Wrap music.

This type of dress is never able to be worn.

Address.

What has a horn but it unable to honk?

A rhino.

Who's there?
Ben and Anna.
Ben and Anna who?
Ben and Anna split
with a cherry on top!

Who's there?
Who.
Who who?
Who the one you're
talking to?

She saw Sheriff's shoes on the sofa.
But was she so sure she saw
Sheriff's shoes on the sofa?

Why is it so windy inside a stadium?

There are hundreds of fans.

Why do vampires seem sick?

They're always coffin.

What did the snowman ask the other snowman?

Do you smell carrots?

This can clap but has no hands.
Thunder.

RIDDLES

Billy was asked to paint numbers on apartments 1 through 100. How many times will he have to paint the number 8?

20 times (8, 18, 28, 38, 48, 58, 68, 78, 80, 81, 82, 83, 84, 85, 86, 87, 88, 89, 98).

Who's there?
Evan.
Evan who?
Evan comes after odd.

Who's there?
Sing.
Sing who?
Whoooooo!

Through three cheese trees
three free fleas flew.
While these fleas flew,
freezy breeze blew.
Freezy breeze made
these three trees freeze.
Freezy trees made
these trees' cheese freeze.
That's what made
these three free fleas sneeze.

TONGUE TWISTER

Why can't you trust zookeepers?

They love cheetahs.

What did Jack say to Jill after they rolled down the hill?

"I think I spilled the water."

How many seconds are there in a year?

Twelve (January 2nd, February 2nd, March 2nd...).

RIDDLES

How do you make the odd number seven even without addition, subtraction, multiplication, or division?

Remove the letter "S."

Knock Knock!

Who's there?
Lettuce.
Lettuce who?
Lettuce in!

Knock Knock!

Who's there?
A tish.
A tish who?
Bless you.

Four furious friends fought for the phone.

Black background, brown background.

What's red and bad for your teeth?

A brick.

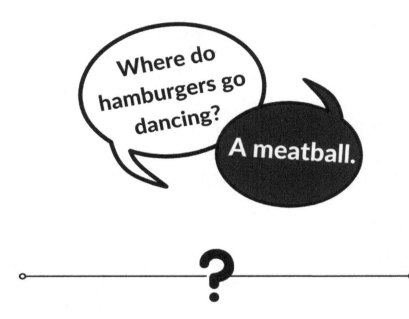

Where do hamburgers go dancing?

A meatball.

The more of this there is, the less you see. What is it?
Darkness.

RIDDLES

What continues to go up and down without moving?
Stairs.

Knock Knock!

Who's there?
Ya.
Ya who?
What are you so excited about?

Knock Knock!

Who's there?
Echo.
Echo who?
Echo who? Echo who?

Seven slick slimey snakes slowly sliding southward.

Roofs of mushrooms rarely mush too much.

What do you call a cow with no legs?

Ground beef!

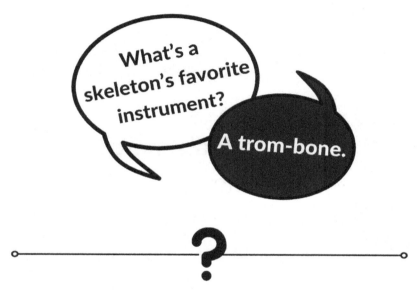

What's a skeleton's favorite instrument?

A trom-bone.

?

If you're running in a race and you pass the person in second place, what place are you now in?

Second place.

RIDDLES

There is a word that could be written forward, backward, or upsidedown and can still be read left to right. What is the word?

NOON.

Knock Knock!

Who's there?
You'll.
You'll who?
You'll never know
until you open the door!

Knock Knock!

Who's there?
Me.
Me who?
Wow! You don't know
who you are?

I wish to wash my Irish wristwatch.

TONGUE TWISTER

On a lazy laser raiser lies a laser ray eraser.

What did Aquaman say to his kids when they wouldn't eat their food?

"Water you waiting for?"

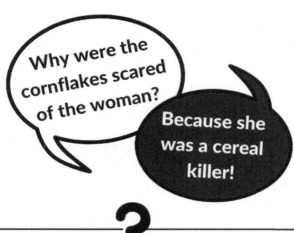

Why were the cornflakes scared of the woman?

Because she was a cereal killer!

?

What is at the end of everything?
The letter "g".

RIDDLES

What has many words but is never able to speak?
A book.

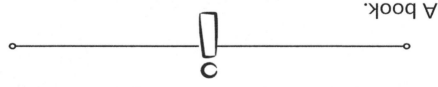

⟶ DID YOU KNOW? ⟵

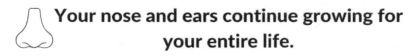
Your nose and ears continue growing for your entire life.

Who's there?

Zee.

Zee who?

Can't you zee I'm knocking?!

Knock Knock!

Who's there?

Claire.

Claire who?

Claire out the room!

Knock Knock!

Eddie edited it.

The ruddy widow really wants ripe watermelon and red roses when winter arrives.

What's the best thing to put into a pie?

Your teeth.

How do modern-day pirates keep in touch?

SEA-mail.

What runs in the backyard but never actually moves?

A fence.

RIDDLES

DID YOU KNOW?

 Frogs drink water through their skin.

How many sheets could a sheet slitter slit if a sheet slitter could slit sheets?

Sounding by sound is a sound method of sounding sounds.

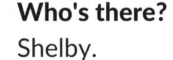

Knock Knock!

Who's there?
Tennis.
Tennis who?
Tennis is five plus five!

Knock Knock!

Who's there?
Shelby.
Shelby who?
She'll be coming around the mountain!

Where do horses live?

In neighhh-borhoods.

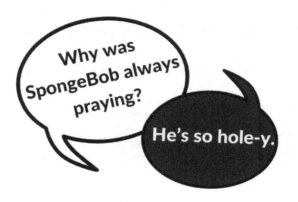

Why was SpongeBob always praying?

He's so hole-y.

What did the shark say when he ate the clownfish?

"This tastes a little funny."

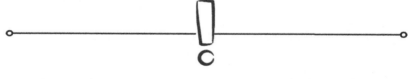

--☰ DID YOU KNOW? ☰--

 Owls can't move their eyeballs.

Neptune's days are 16 hours long.

Salty broccoli, salty broccoli, salty broccoli

A slimy snake slithered down the sandy Sahara.

Who's there?
Water.
Water who?
Water you doing in my house!?

Who's there?
Etch.
Etch who?
Bless you!

What's the most expensive kind of fish?

A gold fish.

What's scarier than a monster?

A momster.

What did one block say to the other when he was ready to leave the party?

"LEGO."

-‑:̲ DID YOU KNOW? :̲‑--

It's impossible to sneeze with your eyes open.

Your brain is 70% water.

Will you, William?
Will you, William?
Will you, William?
Can't you, don't you,
won't you, William?

Five frantic frogs fled from
fifty fierce fishes.

Knock
Knock!

Who's there?
Anee.
Anee who?
Anee one you like!

Knock
Knock!

Who's there?
Otto.
Otto who?
Otto know. I forgot.

Which hand is better to paint with?

Neither! A paint brush is better.

Why does the moon say she doesn't want to eat?

"She's full."

What goes up but doesn't come back down?

Your age.

-:- DID YOU KNOW? -:-

One of the smallest dinosaurs ever was the Compsognathus, which was about the size of a chicken.

**The owner of the outside inn
was inside his outside inn.**

Dust is a disk's worst enemy.

Who's there?
Isabel.
Isabel who?
Isabel working?

Who's there?
Robin.
Robin who?
Robin you.
Give me your money!

Who gives sharks presents on Christmas?

Santa Jaws.

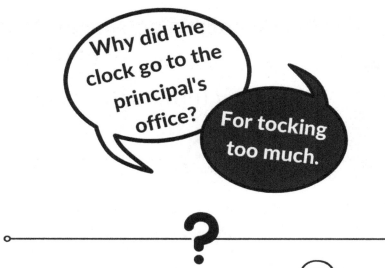
Why did the clock go to the principal's office?

For tocking too much.

What is so fragile that saying its name breaks it?
Silence.

RIDDLES

People make me, save me, change me, and raise me. What am I?
Money.

What runs through towns and over hills but never moves?
A road.

Why was the cookie sad?

Because his mom was a wafer so long.

What do knights do when they are scared of the dark?

They turn on the night light!

Who's there?
Cow says.
Cow says who?
No, a cow says mooooo!

Who's there?
Hawaii.
Hawaii who?
I'm good. Hawaii you?

When do you go in red and stop on green?

When you are eating a watermelon.

Cooks cook cupcakes quickly.

Red lorry, yellow lorry.

Green glass globes glow greenly.

What instrument can you hear but never see?
Your voice.

What has a neck without a head to hold?
A bottle.

What do you call a boomerang that won't come back?

A stick.

What do planets like to read?

Comet books!

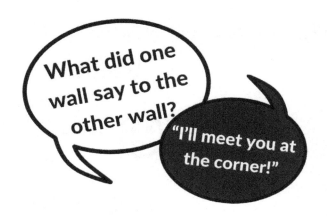

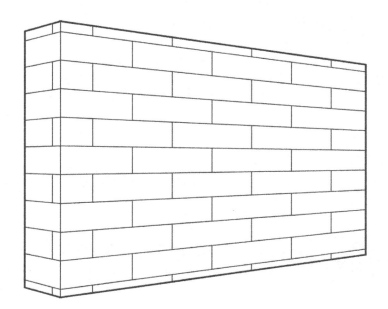

I looked right at Larry's rally and left in a hurry.

The big bug bit the little beetle.

Who's there?
Iran.
Iran who?
Iran here. I'm tired!

Who's there?
Ice cream.
Ice cream who?
Ice cream if you don't give me some candy!